DATE DUE

An art museum might seem quiet and calm, but behind the "Staff Only" doors it can be a high-pitched scene. Walk among the workrooms at the National Gallery of Art, where curators, guards, carpenters, engineers, and over 90,000 works of art await the events of the day.

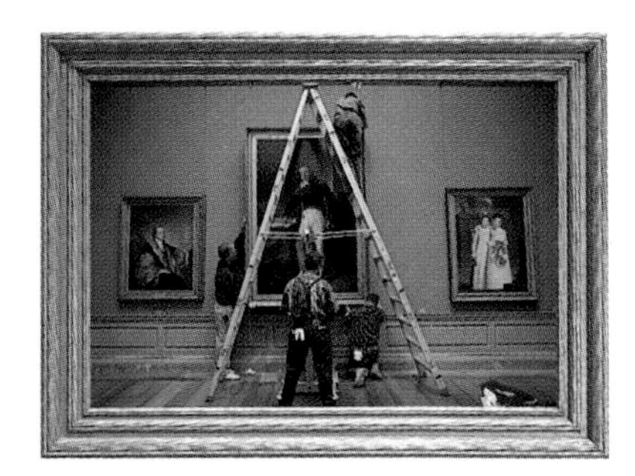

HOUGHTON MIFFLIN COMPANY, BOSTON

NATIONAL GALLERY OF ART, WASHINGTON

1997

The Nine-Ton Cat

Behind the Scenes at an Art Museum

BY PEGGY THOMSON WITH BARBARA MOORE

EDITED BY CAROL ERON

ACKNOWLEDGMENTS

This book is dedicated to the love of art, which draws most museum staff to their professions. We wish to thank Earl A. Powell III, director, Linda Downs, head of education, and Frances P. Smyth, editor-in-chief, at the National Gallery of Art for sustaining an atmosphere of challenge and creativity. Almost every department gave something important to the book after its inception under Kathy Walsh-Piper. The curators, design staff, conservation labs, educators, exhibition staff, registrars, photography and imaging departments, research and archives staff, library, security force, operations division, framers, engineers, art handlers, and horticulturists went an extra mile to explain details of their jobs and to find ways to illustrate them. Last, photographic research and tracking and organizing manuscript drafts were handled expertly by Anne Zapletal.

This book is made possible by a grant from the VIRA I. HEINZ ENDOWMENT

Published by
Houghton Mifflin Company
222 Berkeley Street
Boston, Massachusetts 02116

In association with the
National Gallery of Art
Washington, D.C. 20565

For information about this and other Houghton Mifflin trade and reference books and multimedia products, visit The Bookstore at Houghton Mifflin on the World Wide Web at http://www.hmco.com/trade/.

Design: Margaret Bauer
Type is set in Berkeley Oldstyle and Myriad

Library of Congress
Cataloging-in-Publication Data

Thomson, Peggy.

The nine-ton cat: behind the scenes at an art museum / by Peggy Thomson with Barbara Moore; edited by Carol Eron.

p. cm.

Summary: A behind-the-scenes look at the National Gallery of Art including its private spaces, workshops, offices, and labs where visitors rarely enter.

ISBN 0-395-82655-1 (hardcover)
ISBN 0-395-82683-7 (pbk.)

1. National Gallery of Art (U.S.)—Juvenile literature. [1. National Gallery of Art (U.S.)] I. Moore, Barbara. II. Eron, Carol. III. Title.

N856.T48 1997
708.153—dc20 96-18809 CIP AC

Printed in United States of America
HOR 10 9 8 7 6 5 4 3 2 1

Six a.m.

Without a flashlight the guard knows his way among the shadowy unmoving figures, the bronze statues in the sculpture hall. Silent fountains, not yet turned on, puddle in their gigantic marble saucers. The only sounds are the guard's steps and a distant whine of vacuum cleaners.

Elsewhere in the museum creatures are stirring, for the hours before 10 a.m., when the doors will open to the public, are busy. The two massive buildings of this museum, the National Gallery of Art in Washington—which stretch almost a third of a mile from one end to the other, hold over 90,000 paintings, drawings, and other works of art to be cared for and studied. There are exhibitions to be put up and taken down, acres of marble and oak floors to be polished, food prepared for hungry visitors, tours and activities for children to be planned, sculpture scrubbed, paintings counted, doors unlocked.

Gloved art handlers on ladders lift down two paintings and hang others in their place. Then two more, and a fifth. They move almost every picture in the room before the curator in charge pronounces it ready for the public.

Nearby, in a long marble hall, gardeners shake the trunks of indoor trees and sweep up fallen leaves, they water and feed plants and trundle batches of tired fig trees, palms, orchid and lily plants back to the greenhouses.

From the electricians' shop, a "lamper" pushes out a yellow cart and starts her rounds. The cart holds an electric lift that raises her 30 feet high to replace light-bulbs in the soaring ceilings. She works full-time checking the museum's 8,000 lights.

She and the guard greet each other in passing. From a balcony in the rotunda, the lamper sees an engineer below switching on the fountain. With a wooden shepherd's crook, he wets the rim of the fountain so that water will not cut grooves into the stone, but will spill evenly over the edges.

At a loading dock deep inside the museum, paintings for a new exhibition arrive in crates from around the world. Upstairs, carpenters, painters, and electricians—all with rolling workbenches, scaffolds, and carts—prepare galleries for the show. Amid the clutter and noise, order is emerging, and a pleased-looking man paces the rooms. "Prowling," he calls it. The museum director, who has arrived well before his first meeting of the day, watches the new exhibition take shape. Watching is the director's privilege, he says, and his job.

10

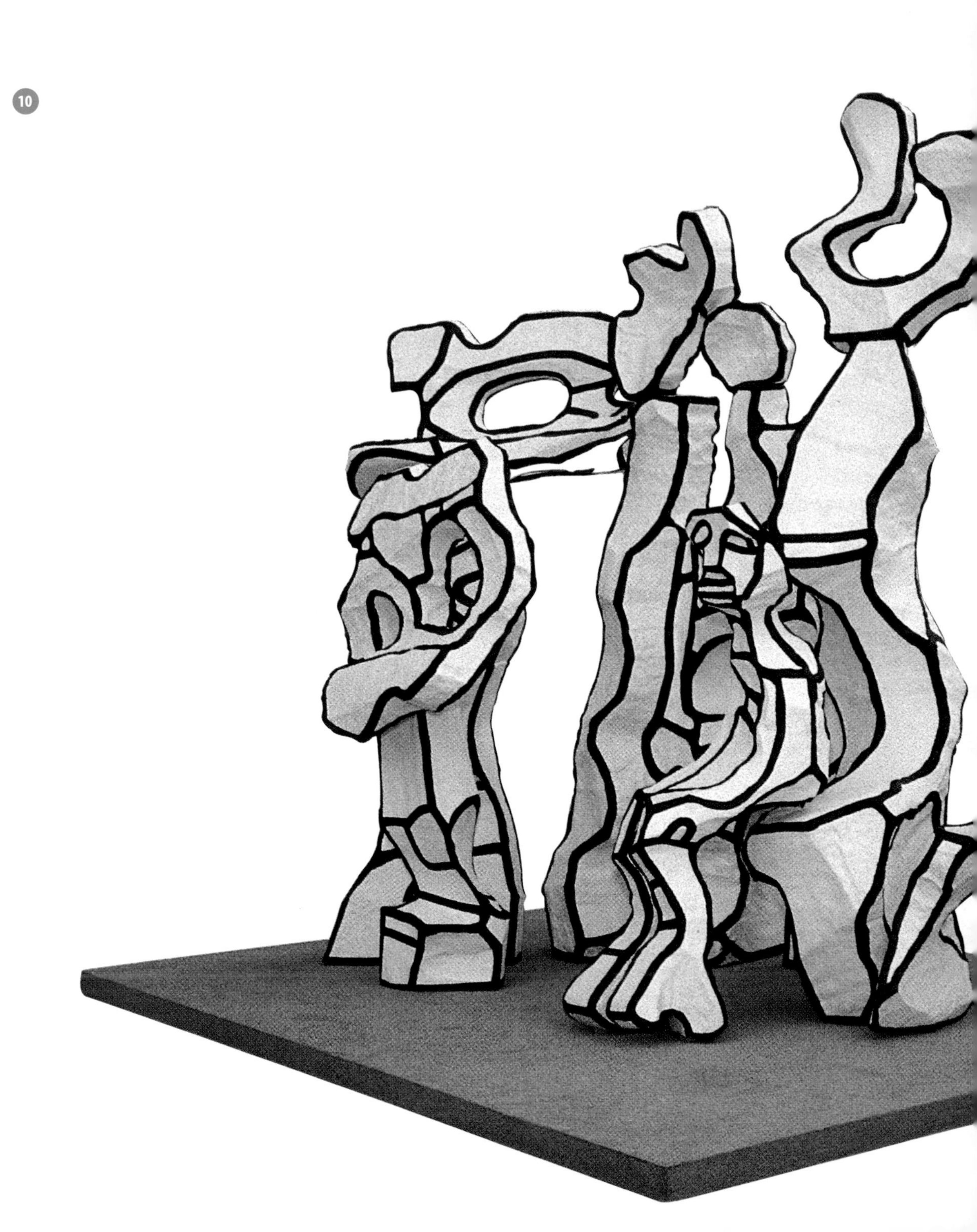

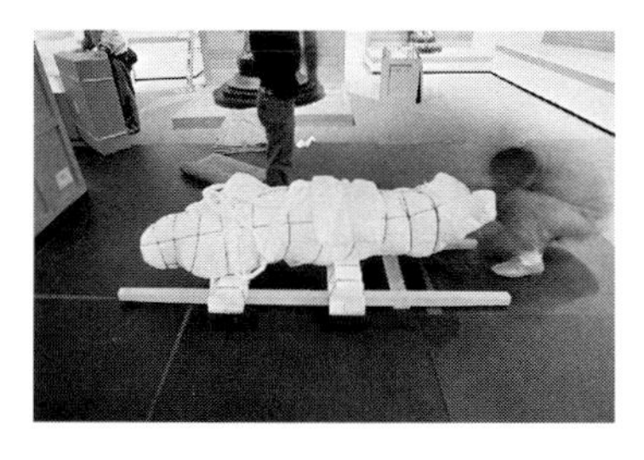

The lamper has made good time. She flicks switches, lighting the public spaces all over the museum. Crossing the underground link between the museum's West and East buildings, she checks the lights on a waterfall which splashes down from a fountain above. By the time she reaches the East Building, sunlight from the glass frame roof throws a patchwork of triangles and stripes on the vast marble wall at the entrance.

At 9:45, the guards take their posts, awaiting the electronic signal to unlock the front doors and greet the first visitors of the day, now gathering outside. They arrive mostly on foot, but also in buses, cars, limos, taxis, vans, wheelchairs, and strollers. Staffers still working in the galleries and public hallways finish their jobs. The lamper and her lift vanish through glass doors marked "Staff Only."

1. Curators Are Curious

Each year millions of visitors, sometimes 17,000 in a day, come to see the National Gallery's works of art. The 94,000 paintings, sculpture, medals, works on paper, and decorative arts from Europe, America, and the Far East include works by all the great masters from the Renaissance to modern times. Leonardo da Vinci, Titian, Raphael, Rembrandt, Vermeer, Manet, Cassatt, Monet, Cézanne, Gauguin, Homer, and Picasso are among the artists whose works can be seen.

Many museums, like the National Gallery, are actually a collection of collections of art. The keepers of the art are curators—from the Latin *curare,* meaning "to care." They care for and study the works of art. Through research, which can require years spent in libraries and museums, they expand their knowledge about the collections. Their work also requires conferring with other experts and knowledge of works of art in auction houses, churches, palaces, and artists' studios throughout the world.

Caring for and evaluating original works of art, like this print by American artist Roy Lichtenstein, are part of curatorial work.

With experience, the curator develops an informed "eye," a set of visual images that helps in distinguishing variations in brushwork, color, texture, and composition, among artists and within an artist's own works. The curator's specialized visual skills and research are useful as well in developing the museum's collections. The curator builds breadth by bringing in works from an important period not previously represented, and achieves greater depth by adding works of an artist or group of artists already well represented. A curator might recommend purchasing a painting at auction, or find and arrange the purchase of a sculpture from a private source, or, as is often the case, encourage owners to give them as gifts. At the National Gallery of Art there are 29 curators, each with a specialty.

In his book-filled office the curator of French art studies a photograph of a painting: a portrait of a man and his hunting dog by an 18th-century French artist, Jean-Baptiste Oudry. The curator is happy because he has been on a search, hoping to add to the museum's extensive collection of French paintings. He traveled to New York, London, and Paris to study museum and private collections, visited colleagues and friends in the art world, and hunted through the storerooms of art dealers. The picture he now studies became available through a New York dealer who acquired it in France. The painting is not only beautiful but historically important, as it depicts the master of the hunt for King Louis XV of France. The hunt master, the curator says, brought the artist Jean-Baptiste Oudry to the court, and the king invited him to paint royal hunt scenes and a series of portraits of the king's dogs. The painting itself is now in a large crate on a ship coming from France. In his mind's eye, the curator already sees it hanging on a certain wall in the museum.

When the portrait arrives, the curator describes the new purchase to the owner of another painting by Oudry. This one depicts a pair of the king's lively dogs, a greyhound and a setter eyeing each other sharply. It would be a wonderful complement to the new acquisition. The owner has promised it as a future gift to the museum, but meanwhile, the curator inquires, would he lend it for a show? The owner decides to make it a gift now, and so two important additions to the collection—one a purchase, the other a gift—hang side by side in the museum.

Top: Jean-Baptiste Oudry, ***The Marquis de Beringhen***

Bottom: Jean-Baptiste Oudry, ***Misse and Luttine***

eronymus Bosch, *Death and the Miser*

A large part of a curator's job is to research art already in the museum's collections. One example is *Death and the Miser* by Hieronymus Bosch, which the curator of Northern Renaissance art studies for its iconography, that is, the meaning of the painting in its own time.

A dying man is depicted in a narrow bed. A skeleton has entered, carrying the arrow of death, and beside him a toad-faced demon offers a sack of money. Across the bed an angel directs the man's gaze to a crucifix in the window. At his moment of death, the painting asks, will the miser choose to go with angels or demons?

To understand further, the curator investigates ideas about good and evil in Dutch society of the artist's time. Bosch and others believed that death involved a series of struggles between good and evil, and the details in his painting represent these forces at work on the miser.

The curator also studies symbols in the painting—the angel, representing salvation; the demon, temptation; and the skeleton, death. But other elements are more difficult. Careful analysis tells the curator that the figure at the foot of the bed is presented as evil and two-faced: with one hand he greedily drops money in a chest, while with the other he fingers rosary beads.

The miser himself, facing death, reaches out his hand. Infrared images of the panel (reflectograms) reveal that under the paint Bosch originally drew the dying man clutching money and possessions. But in the final painting the artist changed his mind, and as the dying man stares at death, his hands are empty.

Thus the artist chose to leave the miser's fate hanging in the balance so that the viewer, together with the miser, must choose: heaven or hell?

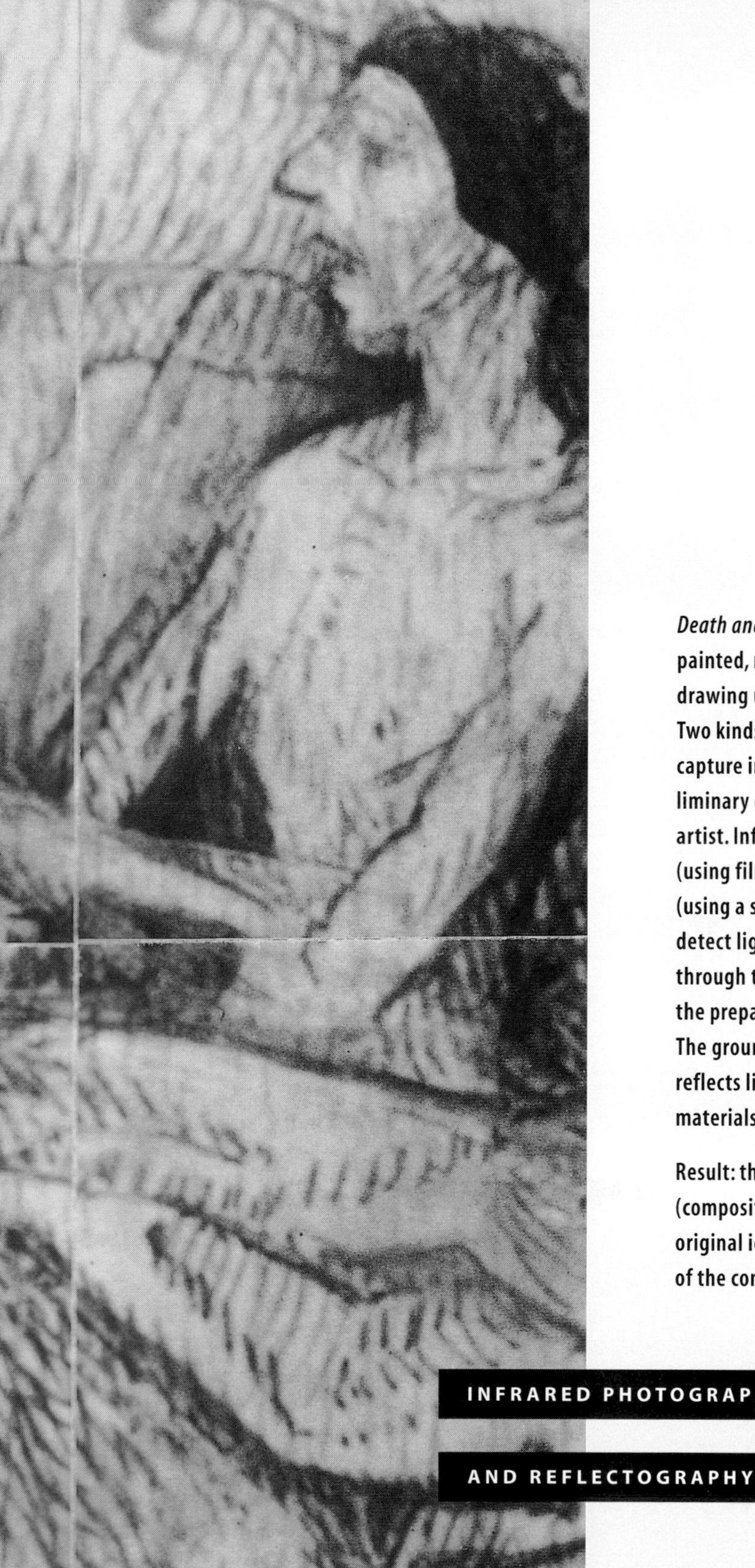

Death and the Miser is thinly painted, revealing that there is drawing under its surface. Two kinds of imaging techniques capture in detail these pre-liminary drawings made by the artist. Infrared photography (using film) and reflectography (using a special video camera) detect light that has penetrated through the paint layers to the preparation, or ground, layer. The ground, which is white, reflects light, while the drawing materials absorb light.

Result: the infrared reflectogram (composite), left, shows the artist's original ideas. At far left, a detail of the completed painting.

INFRARED PHOTOGRAPHY AND REFLECTOGRAPHY

Curator, designers, and museum director discuss plans for a Gauguin exhibition. At right, a pair of wooden shoes that Paul Gauguin carved, painted, and then wore with an embroidered Breton vest and his hair long, causing a sensation in Paris

Curators are also responsible for developing the museum's special exhibitions. They first must present their ideas to the museum's director and the exhibition committee for approval. If they can convince the committee that the show is a good idea, and if funds are available or can be raised to pay for it, then dates are scheduled, often a year to five or more in advance. It can take that long to complete the research, select art from around the world, arrange for its loan, write the catalogue, ship the art to the museum, and install the show.

The concept for an exhibition may begin with a date—the world in 1492 as seen through a vast gathering of works of art, maps, scientific instruments, and books from that time. It may be an in-depth look at a single painting—discoveries revealed in Jan van Eyck's newly restored *Annunciation*—or the idea may be the work of a single artist.

An exhibition on Paul Gauguin related the National Gallery's collection of this late 19th-century French artist's work to his entire career. The museum has over 150 of Gauguin's paintings, prints, ceramics, and sculpture—even a pair of wooden shoes that the artist carved, painted, and wore. To create the exhibition, the museum collaborated with the Art Institute of Chicago and the Musée d'Orsay in Paris, which both have strong Gauguin collections as well.

"An exhibition is like a play in several acts," says a curator. "Visitors need to sense this structure or they may feel lost." In this case, the curators decide to display Gauguin's work chronologically, with certain groupings by subject. They plan one section to focus on Gauguin's years in the coastal farm region of Brittany, where he searched for a simple, authentic existence as a subject for his art. For a later section they choose works Gauguin made in Tahiti, where he perfected his bold, intense style in images of the island's people and daily life.

With this plan in mind, the curators work with the museum's designers on floor plans and scale-model rooms, using tiny replicas of Gauguin's work to organize the layout of the show.

A month before the opening, the works of art arrive. The registrar logs them in, then the conservators and curators examine them to verify their condition and check for any possible damage suffered during travel. Specialized museum staff, the art handlers, place the works in the rooms for the show, according to plans.

"Then we start over again," says a curator. "The objects we thought about hanging side by side may have looked fine on the walls of the model, but in full size on the walls they may not work at all. We often shift everything around."

In the course of their work curators become detectives, as in the case of a legendary missing painting. It was an enormous Swiss mountain scene, *Lake Lucerne*, by Albert Bierstadt, who had studied art in Europe and later became famous for his paintings of the American West. *Lake Lucerne* had been missing for more than a century. As the curators planned the exhibition about the life and works of Bierstadt, they pondered its whereabouts.

"We knew from written accounts that Bierstadt exhibited *Lake Lucerne* in New York in 1858, and that a man in Rhode Island bought the painting in 1882," says a curator of American art. "It's a very large painting, pretty hard to slip under a bed and forget about. Maybe it had been destroyed and we'd never see it. That was hard to accept, because we knew how important it was to Bierstadt. It summed up everything he'd learned in Europe and contained the seeds of the paintings he would later produce when he traveled west. It represented a major turning point for him."

Without this painting, the exhibition would have a major gap. There was not even a photograph or a drawing of *Lake Lucerne,* only newspaper accounts from people who had seen it. Preparations for the exhibition were nearly complete and the catalogue for the exhibition was written and ready to be printed when a phone call came from Rhode Island, saying that a woman who had owned a huge painting had died. In going through her house the woman's lawyers had found the painting with *A. Bierstadt* inscribed in the right hand corner.

One curator remembers holding her breath when the painting was described as a large "western" scene with covered wagons. When she heard that the date 1858 was written in the corner, she thought there was only one picture it could be. The "covered wagons" were actually gypsy wagons, and the mountainous setting was Switzerland.

The curators rushed to Rhode Island to see *Lake Lucerne.* In its gilt frame it measured 12 feet across. It had been purchased in the 1890s, they learned, and later reportedly lowered into a new house before the roof was completed. To get it out again required cutting an opening in the side of the house, then hoisting the painting out and into a truck. Several months thereafter, with funds from two donors, the National Gallery purchased the painting at auction. All the curators agreed: such luck as the discovery of *Lake Lucerne* was wonderful, but rare.

The painting had not been cared for in a long time, so a museum conservator worked feverishly to ready it for the exhibition. While he cleaned it, the museum buzzed with daily bulletins on his progress. As the discolored old varnish was removed, the curator was called to see how the tiny clock face on the village church had emerged. "The day before it was just a murky area," she remembers. "Now the hands pointed to two o'clock." Bierstadt left this message for the keenest viewers.

Albert Bierstadt, *Lake Lucerne*

Munch
Symbols and Images
20TH CENTURY MASTERS
THE THYSSEN-BORNEMISZA COLLECTION
Visions of City & Country
David Smith
Mauritshuis
Dutch Painting of the Golden Age
中華人民共和

2. The Paintings Make the Rules

In the design studio, pencils scrape across paper and electric erasers buzz. Architects, graphic artists, and a lighting designer are sketching plans for where paintings will hang, where sculpture will stand, and especially how the art will be seen.

The objective is to create settings with a sense of place and time that draw connections between the works of art and the themes that inspired their creation. When planning for an exhibition, designers work with the curators to consider the artists, their lives and times, and how their work was intended to be viewed. Would a painting have hung in a large church, or in an intimate setting, such as the library of a private house?

At drafting tables the designers draw freely at first, then in fine detail. Later they work with miniature reproductions of paintings and sculpture, called maquettes, and they select architectural elements and other design details for the new exhibits.

The design team's work space is both open and crowded. Narrow paths link the drafting tables, and surfaces are cluttered with rolls of drawing paper, pots of pencils, pens, and brushes, and models—of a Shaker barn, a Japanese teahouse, windows from a British country house—reminders of bygone exhibitions. In this studio the grand spaces of the museum are contemplated, and they serve as a guide. But ultimately, a designer says, "The paintings make the rules. They tell us how to present what is moving and magnificent about them."

When an exhibition is in the process of being installed, museum designers often work late. In the design studio: maquettes (tiny stand-up paper models) and drawings for the exhibition *Circa 1492*

Before it was installed on a ceiling, Titian's *Saint John the Evangelist on Patmos* hung on a gallery wall. "You'd see this dramatic, swirling figure," recalls a member of the design staff. "Saint John, twisted, with scarcely any ground under him, and vast sky all around. It was disorienting. Was he falling?"

Titian, who had made the painting for the ceiling of a religious fraternity in Venice, created it to be seen from afar, by people looking up as they entered a dimly lit room. In the work, Saint John is startled by a vision of God and angels and hears a great voice telling him to write down what he has seen. In a gesture of awe, his eyes fixed on heaven, he thrusts upward, flinging his arms wide. The eagle beside him, a symbol of the saint, is startled, too, and stares in the same direction.

The designers wanted to recapture something of the original setting so the painting would make more sense to modern visitors. To do so, designers and curators researched in books and traveled to Venice, where they climbed high among the beams and supports of 16th-century ceilings. Back at the museum all agreed: "We thought that this painting needed to be seen from underneath and at an angle, as it was originally."

A scaffolding was built for the designers and carpenters who created the complex paneled ceiling. After art handlers bolted the painting in place, it was lit softly from beneath to approximate the viewer's experience of 500 years ago.

A ceiling was built for Titian's painting of Saint John. Construction and installation were done from a scaffold and a hydraulic lift. Left, the completed installation

For David Smith's modern steel sculpture, the staff also attempted to evoke the artist's intent. Smith had displayed 26 of these works, from the Voltri series, in an ancient Roman amphitheater in Spoleto, Italy. When National Gallery curators later chose to show a special group of them, the designers called for stepped terraces to suggest the amphitheater. As a result, the sunlit upper level of the museum's contemporary East Building was transformed into a space that seemed both ancient and modern, where people could wander freely among the sculpture.

The setting also echoed the different ground levels at the artist's studio in Bolton Landing, New York, where Smith set his sculpture on a deck and in the surrounding fields to become part of the landscape. Smith placed some of the pieces, which he called Sentinels, at the side of a pond with the forest and mountains beyond. Later installed in the museum's Tower Room, ramrod-straight *Sentinel V* stands aloof in a high corner, keeping watch over the other sculpture.

Four hundred years separate Titian's *Saint John* from Smith's work, but each is at home in the space created for it. The Titian, in low artificial light, remains the same every season, while the Smith sculpture, under a skylight, reflects the shifts of natural light, from morning to night, and from the blue of a springtime sky to the yellow glow of a winter afternoon.

David Smith first arranged his sculpture on the steps of an ancient theater in Spoleto, Italy.

Later, museum designers, working at right on a scale model, created a room that echoes the outdoor mood of the original setting.

COLOR, COLOR ON THE WALL

Wall colors in the museum are selected to enhance the art.

In the room of David Smith's sculpture, all the walls are white, and the steps are textured like stone — an effect achieved by mixing grit into the paint, to suggest a sandstone amphitheater.

Pale yellow, the color the artist himself preferred, sets off portraits and scenes of London by James McNeill Whistler.

The portrait of *The Washington Family,* painted by Edward Savage in 1796, hangs against a gray-blue that was favored in the period.

PLEXI; THRESHOLD EDGE
SCALE 1½" = 1'-0"
PLEXI; THRESHOLD EDGE
SECTION TO CO
SCALE 1½" = 1
PAN WON'T FIT
20½" × 17" × 5½" Ht.
ROOM 4 NORTH WEST CORNER

Every year the museum presents several dozen special exhibitions, which usually include works of art borrowed from other museums and private collectors. They are temporary shows, lasting three to six months, but take years to plan.

In the towers of the National Gallery's East Building, only the outer walls of the exhibition rooms, called pods, are permanent. For every new exhibition, a new plan and design are made, and crews of carpenters, painters, electricians, and drywall finishers transform the spaces.

Sometimes bare walls are best for an exhibition, but not for treasures from British country houses. In this case, interior elements of the houses were recreated to present the armor, porcelain, rare books, landscapes, portraits of royalty and beloved horses, and sculpture collected by British nobility. The heart of this show was the 18th-century passion for collecting and displaying art in the halls and galleries of these grand houses.

In English country houses, the fireplace was often the focus of attention. For the special exhibition *Treasure Houses of Britain*, designers drew plans from several fireplaces to create an ideal corner setting in the museum, for antique porcelains and silver andirons.

Working from actual examples, the designers chose elements such as a window, the shape of a room, a door frame, and the custom of hanging pictures vertically, one above the other on high walls. Craftspeople were added to the team to weave wall coverings, print wallpaper, paint wood to resemble old walnut paneling, and "marbleize" columns of plaster.

The designers transformed the very space where the David Smith sculpture had stood into the family portrait and heirloom gallery of a historic country house, even disguising the skylights as a vaulted ceiling. The huge formal room was dazzling. With alcoves at both ends, separated from the main area by classical columns, it was the kind of room where collectors would have shown their old master paintings, acquired on grand tours abroad.

In a later rebuilding of that same area, designers turned the space into a Spanish turret with high Moorish windows, for an exhibition of art at the time Columbus arrived in America. A year later the space was again transformed, to honor the paintings of Pablo Picasso, all before the Smith sculpture was reinstalled.

CLAWS AND CLIPS

Invisibility is the goal of the bracket maker who fashions the claws and clips that hold small works of art firmly, yet delicately, in place while on exhibit. He smooths the fasteners so that sharp edges do not catch the light, and he paints them to match whatever they hold, be it wood, porcelain, clay, or metal.

The materials used are of greatest importance. "If you have an object made of lead, and its brackets are iron and they're cushioned with wool felt — fine, you might think," explains the bracket maker. "But close it up in a case and the chemical reaction will rot the lead and turn it to powder!" In this example, he uses polyester felt and brass or steel.

Lighting a museum is a problem. There must not be too little or too much light, and what is right in one area is wrong in another. With good lighting a visitor can see more detail in a painting or an object. But light can gravely damage the art, fading colors and causing materials to disintegrate. So a lighting designer monitors light levels in the galleries with both people and the art in mind.

"At the entry doors, we want strong light for people coming in from the street, so they don't trip and fall," says the designer. "Then we take people through a series of transitions into darker spaces so that their eyes can adjust."

"The Nine-Ton Cat"
A stepped pyramid inspired by Aztec temples was built to distribute the weight of a huge stone jaguar, dramatically lit, at the entrance to a show of Aztec art.

But even in the darkest galleries people can always glimpse more light ahead in the next room, and this is inviting: like a lamp in the window, when you're coming home.

How much light to use? On a clear day outside the museum, on Washington's grassy Mall, a light meter registers about 8,000 foot candles, a foot candle being the amount of light from a candle burning one foot away. Inside the museum, paintings are lit at 30 foot candles, and especially light-sensitive pieces such as drawings are lit at 5 foot candles or less.

The lighting designer chooses bulbs (he calls them lamps) from among hundreds of possibilities, selecting them for color as well as for their intensity in foot candles. Each work of art has its own requirements. Consider sculpture. "If you want to show the shape of a sculpture, as it is seen in the gallery when natural light streams through the skylight," says the designer, "a broad overall light is needed, while a tight beam illuminates details of the sculptor's modeling. Shadows are also important, and in the wrong place they can produce an effect contrary to what the artist desired."

Many decisions were made in lighting the following objects:

A rare treasure from the Middle Ages, the Chalice of the Abbot Suger of Saint-Denis, is lit from above and from four directions, so that light glows from the silver, gold, and gems and shines through the thin sardonyx sides of the cup. Wherever a viewer stands, the reflection of the chalice can be seen on its glass case. The cup is set on a raised pedestal, as if it has been lifted, so that the cup's shadows form a cross on the floor.

Field Painting by Jasper Johns produces its own light and requires an electrical outlet for its neon sign. R, the neon says, for red, in one of the artist's playful comments on names and meanings.

If the light for Verrocchio's clay bust of *Lorenzo de' Medici* came from directly above, or even from a single angle, the shadowy face would menace. But Lorenzo, known as the Magnificent, was a poet, politician, and patron of the arts in Renaissance Italy, and despite his tough, crooked nose and jutting jaw, his eyes are thoughtful. To do him justice, the designer positions the lamps at a distance and from several directions to fully illuminate Lorenzo's strong,

Left to right: Chalice of the Abbot Suger of Saint-Denis; Jasper Johns, *Field Painting;* Andrea del Verrocchio, *Lorenzo de' Medici* and *Putto Poised on a Globe;* Henri Matisse, *La Négresse*

Putto Poised on a Globe, also by Verrocchio, would suffer from overhead lighting. His chubby neck would be lost from sight. Thus he is lit from several angles, including the back, with extra light on his neck.

Because paper is so fragile, Henri Matisse's wall-size paper cutouts are lit by just three- to five-foot candles—among the dimmest anywhere in the museum. The fixtures, mounted on the ceiling, remain on for only half the day. At one o'clock the doors to the room close, and the lights automatically shut off.

3. Conservation Doctors

The only painting by Leonardo da Vinci in America is the portrait he made of Ginevra de' Benci around 1474. Although it is the most popular painting in the National Gallery, *Ginevra* had to be removed from exhibit for cleaning. The varnish on its surface had darkened over 500 years, hiding the beauty of the girl's delicate face. Gallery goers, young and old, scholars and tourists, some from afar, would miss her, but *Ginevra* was gently carried on a padded cart to the painting conservation laboratory—a sort of hospital—for study and treatment.

The lab, a long, hushed room, is equipped with operating room lights, microscopes, and hoses for carrying off chemical fumes. Easels stand by the windows, where conservators work in natural light to restore art to its best possible condition. Within easy reach are their racks of powders and liquids, trays of brushes, swabs, tweezers, and scalpels.

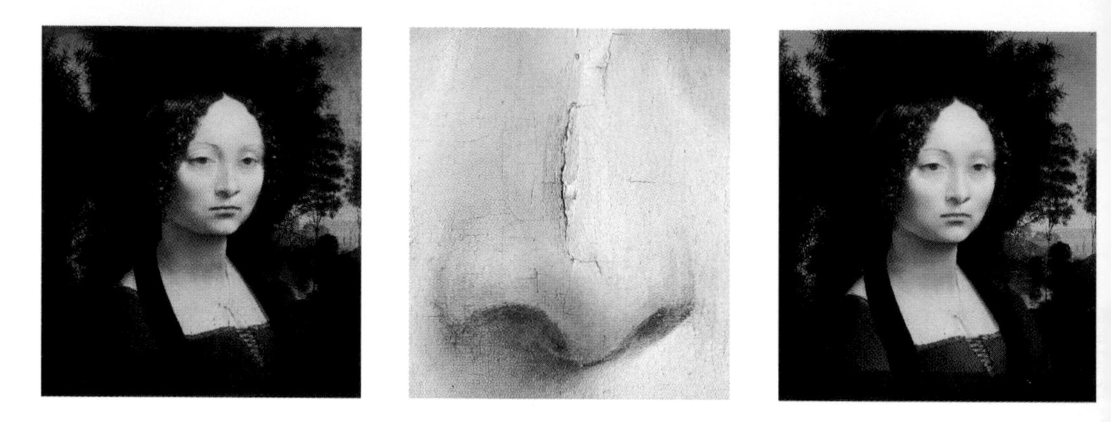

Ginevra de' Benci: **before treatment, damage to the nose (two vertical cracks and six horizontal fissures), and after treatment**

Three months of intensive care were needed before *Ginevra de' Benci* was ready to be hung again in its gallery. During that time, one of the museum's conservators made discoveries that changed what is known about the painting.

At the start of his work, the conservator experienced a magical moment. "You've picked up the painting—very nervously. It's so fragile, 500 years old, so very small. *Ginevra de' Benci* is painted on a thin wood panel. The first impression you get is of the delicacy of her young face. Ginevra is sixteen, perhaps seventeen. She looks at you, and you feel her gentleness.

"We are a bit like doctors, caring for paint ings as if they were our patients," the conservator adds. "They may need major surgery or possibly just a gentle cleaning. The difference is they can't talk, and we've got to find out what's wrong with them."

The conservator's treatment of *Ginevra* depends on his diagnosis. First, he reviews other portraits of women by Leonardo—only two are known: *Mona Lisa* and *Portrait of a Lady with an Ermine*. Studying photographs of *Ginevra*'s "sisters" for clues, he moves from his easel to art history books and back again. The conservator needs not only information, but also familiarity with the painting, the way a doctor must know a patient. For example, he knows that Leonardo originally painted *Ginevra* like the others, as a half-portrait showing her hands, and that the painting was later cut along its lower edge, possibly to remove a damaged area.

The conservator pores over the surface of *Ginevra* with a magnifying loupe and a microscope, through which he sees details magnified 50 times. He studies the painted surface and the condition of the paint, examining every inch for flakes or cracks. As he looks, he also comes to know how Leonardo applied and manipulated paint.

The painting conservation lab. Center, a conservator makes an infrared reflectogram of a painting with camera and computer (page 19). Behind her, conservators examine paintings with microscopes, treat paintings, and study slides of works of art.

Seeing Leonardo's own fingerprint in the painting is almost like standing next to the artist at work.

On a painting, layers of grime accumulate over time and alter its appearance. Cracks develop in the paint, some colors fade, others darken. Varnish, applied to protect the surface and intensify colors (as beach stones look better wet), eventually yellows and can affect the colors below. But under its aged, discolored varnish, he finds *Ginevra* in good condition. Only a few small damages are discovered through x-radiography, at the bridge of her nose and in the sky and the juniper tree behind her.

Next, the conservator confirms that most of the painting had been done in oil. "Leonardo used the palm of his hand and his fingertips to create texture in oil paint and to soften and blend edges. *Ginevra* may be the first example in Italian art of an artist deliberately using his fingers." Up close, these tiny impressions reveal part of Leonardo's fingerprints.

From infrared photography the conservator also discovers that Leonardo worked from a drawing on paper to make the portrait of Ginevra. He used the drawing like a pattern, pricking holes in it along *Ginevra*'s eyes, nose, and chin. Then he placed his drawing on top of the prepared wood panel. Using a cloth bag filled with charcoal powder, he dusted the paper (a process called pouncing) so that the drawing appeared as tiny black dots on the panel. The original drawing is lost, but under infrared light, traces of Leonardo's working method show up as lines of dots around *Ginevra*'s eyes.

Once these examinations are completed, the conservator decides how to proceed with *Ginevra*'s treatment. The most important rule for a conservator is to do as little as possible to a painting. Even though it is safe to remove the dark varnish, he works with great caution. Using small swabs of cotton on slender sticks, he tests tiny areas on the edges of the painting to ensure that the cleaning solvent is gentle enough to dissolve the varnish without affecting the paint. At the upper right, he cleans a tiny spot of the sky. This is a good place to start because he can observe what is happening more clearly on the lighter paints. As he touches a swab to the surface, he gives it a little twist and lifts off the first bit of varnish.

"Everyone in the lab wanted a look," the conservator remembers. "The sky had been a dull green-brown, but there—underneath the cleaned spot—appears one tiny patch of beautiful blue."

"After a few more tests, you start from the edge, and in the same careful way, you move in. You are peeling away centuries of dirt. It's so exciting—seeing Leonardo's brushstrokes and places where he blended the paint with his fingers."

The discolored varnish had made the light colors warmer—the whites yellow, the blues green—and the dark colors lighter. The artist's modeling of the face and the sense of space—what is near and what is far—had flattened. Without the varnish, the colors become stronger and brighter, and depth is restored. At this stage the painting is close to what Leonardo originally intended.

The next step is to protect the original paint by applying a clear modern varnish very thinly with a good pig-bristle brush. Then comes inpainting, which can consume 90 percent of a conservator's time, even though one is only in-painting the areas where paint is missing.

In *Ginevra de' Benci* previous paint losses had been filled in. Luckily the areas are very small—a bit on the nose, in the sky, in the trees, and across the bottom of the painting. The conservator paints in the loss on the bridge of *Ginevra*'s nose, dot by dot, with the finest of sable brushes. What makes it especially hard is matching Leonardo's delicate colors and his subtle modeling while keeping the surface of the paint like his—very thin, never coarse. After inpainting, the conservator applies a thin layer of varnish over these areas as well.

When the portrait goes back on display, one viewer marvels, "Well, the doctor has certainly brought the roses back to her cheeks!"

1.

PULP TO GO

If a hole or tear needs repair, the paper conservation lab can do it. The conservators keep hundreds of types of paper from around the world filed away in drawers. Bits of matching paper are selected, mixed with water in a blender, and used as pulp to fill in the tears and holes.

In the conservation department, different offices are in charge of paintings, sculpture, works of art on paper, textiles, framing, and the scientific research needed to support the work.

In the paper conservation lab, conservators protect and repair drawings, watercolors, and prints. Works on paper are sensitive to light so they often spend time in dark storage. They can turn yellow and brittle with age. They also can develop rusty spots, called foxing, from molds produced in high humidity. Puckers and wrinkles, called cockling, can result from uneven tension where a backing has been pasted on.

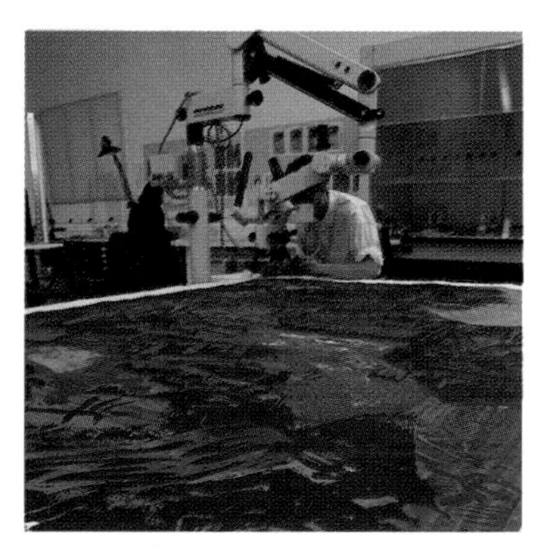

Before treating this large work of art, a conservator studies it through a stereomicroscope, to determine the stability of the paint on the paper surface.

The paper conservators work at high tables and sinks, surrounded by jars of brushes, trays of watercolors and pastels in a rainbow of colors, and paste pots. Monday is paste day here. Paste must be made just so, because it is used to hinge the art to a backing, and it cannot be hurried. A paper conservator stirs a mixture of wheat starch powder and water over a burner, watching it bubble slowly until the white sludge turns gray and translucent.

Nearby, another conservator is treating a drawing.The old paper lining on the back of a Guercino drawing has become brittle and acidic, owing to the nature of the drawing itself. The drawing ink, made from the galls (growths) found on oak trees, becomes very acidic over time. This causes the drawing paper and the lining to break and crack. The lining is therefore removed, and the drawing will be mended with Japanese tissue and paste and relined with a strong mulberry paper to retard further damage by the gall ink.

She sets out three broad brushes for the job:

1. a deer-hair water brush
soft, for dampening the back of the picture

2. a fine horsehair brush
smooth and thin, for applying a narrow strip of paste

3. a palm bristle brush
stiff, for pressing the lining onto the picture and for tapping all across the paper in hard, rhythmic strokes to ensure that the lining sticks

Finally the picture will be dried flat between two pieces of felt.

Conservators, above, repair damage to the black painted surface of a sculpture. Right, work on filling cracks and toning them to match the surface of a Renaissance alabaster statue, *Pietà,* by a 15th-century Netherlandish sculptor.

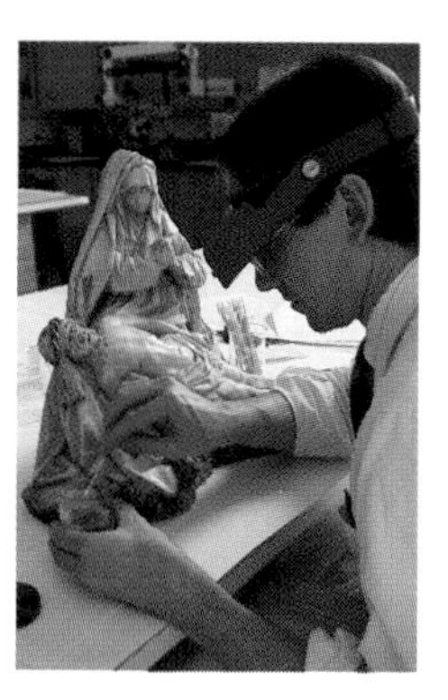

Consider the jobs of conservators who specialize in objects. One day they might be in a fountain with a marble sculpture, and the next day they might be two stories up, scrubbing a monument. Here are some examples.

When tiny silver ornaments on a wooden cabinet from the 1500s blacken from tarnishing, the conservators are called in. The ornaments are removed, one by one, for careful cleaning. When the job is done, the ornaments' amazing details show—right down to the skin and scales on a one-inch-long lizard's back.

A biologist who comes to study the creatures decorating the lid of this cabinet, The Ulrich Coffer, can identify the frogs, crayfish, beetles, and lizards by species and genus. One lizard interests him especially—a wall lizard of the genus *Lacerta*. He sees a break in the patterning of its skin where the tail must have broken off and a new tail grew. Here is evidence that the artist had cast his metal lizard from nature. The silversmith must have covered a lizard with plaster or clay to make a mold, and poured hot metal in the mold to make a perfect silver copy.

A silver lizard, below, and other ornaments were dulled by corrosion when conservators received a rare cabinet, the Ulrich Coffer, for restoration. Once restored, the miniature cabinet gleams with silver and gold against its ebony wood. Inside the bottom drawer, a false back hides a secret compartment.

Outdoor sculpture not only ages but suffers daily exposure to the weather. So Henry Moore's enormous bronze sculpture *Knife Edge,* in front of the National Gallery's East Building, must be cleaned every six months. The conservators climb ladders and use liquid detergent and tap water to scrub its sleek planes with long-handled brushes. It takes four people to buff the sculpture by hand with rags and buffer machines. Once a year they remove the sculpture's protective wax coating and apply a new hard wax to protect against acid rain, dirt, pollen, and bird droppings.

Edgar Degas used light, flexible materials including wine bottle corks, beeswax, and cloth rags to construct his highly experimental wax and clay sculptures, which explore movements such as bending and arching. One figure, *Seated Woman Wiping Her Left Hip,* even contains a salt shaker lid, and an oil lamp wick extends down her lower right side. But Degas' unorthodox combination of materials also made these sculptures fragile. When the artist died in 1917, many of his waxes were found in varying states of collapse and had to be restored, in some cases almost rebuilt, so they could be cast in bronze.

The museum's conservators, who care for a large collection of Degas' wax figures—48 altogether—are engaged in long-term analysis of his sculpture materials and methods of work.

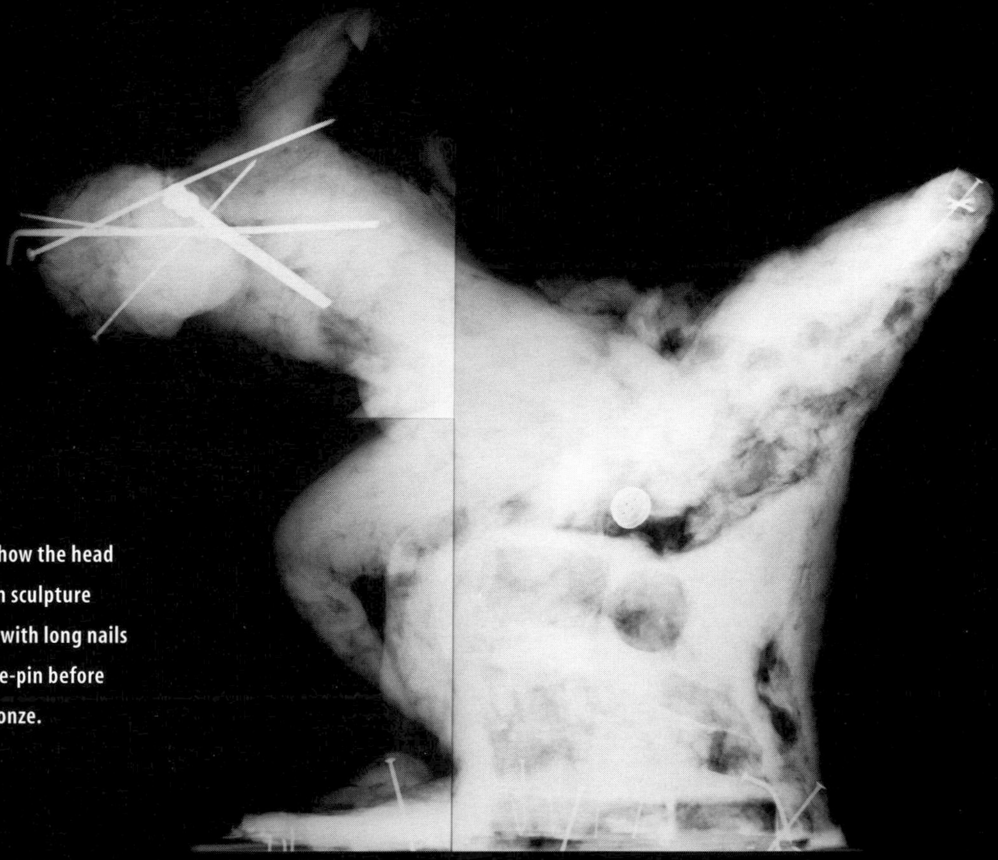

An x-ray shows how the head of Degas' broken sculpture was reattached with long nails and a door hinge-pin before being cast in bronze.

Edgar Degas, *Seated Woman Wiping Her Left Hip*

70 DEGREES AND HUMID

In every exhibition gallery, a small metal box holds a hygrothermo-graph — a delicate metal arm connected to a strand of hair that expands when moisture in the air increases and contracts when it decreases. The arm, with ink stored in its tip, records the very slight changes on a piece of paper coiled around a small drum. On a Monday at 3 p.m. in Gallery 86, the temp-erature is 70 degrees, with humidity at 50 percent — just as it should be.

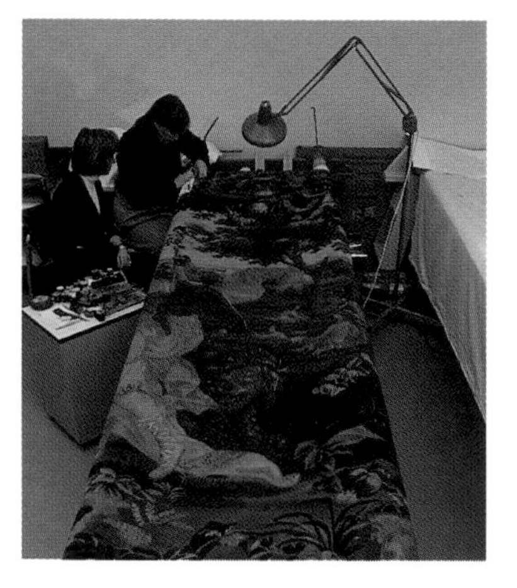

Textile conservators stabilize the top border of an 18th-century Flemish tapestry in preparation for hanging.

Practically all the equipment in the textile conservation lab is white and on wheels. On a white surface, tiny insect droppings will be evident—warning conservators that bugs are on the loose and may be eating a tapestry. In the textile lab insect traps are always set everywhere in the room, on windowsills, in corners, on walls. "Don't laugh," says a textiles conservator. "We number the traps and keep a record of everything we catch in them. Our nightmare would be to see our collection walk away from us on little insect feet."

Before a textile is cleaned or repaired, it is analyzed. The conservator works with solutions, solvents, and specially treated water. "We run eighteen tests on threads taken from the back of the textile. We also run tests for colorfastness on the new threads we will use." Textile conservators keep a rack of threads of every color that have passed the tests and a scorecard for each one. Any of these conservators will admit: it takes finicky people to like this job.

RX FOR WARP THREADS AND SHADOWS

Saints and royalty, richly dressed, more than 70 figures in all, appear on the 500-year-old Mazarin Tapestry. During its long life, threads had broken from the tapestry hanging on its own weight, silver wound around the threads had tarnished, and gold thread had become spotted and crusted. Cleaning it was a massive job.

The front and back of the tapestry were first vacuumed through a protective screening. Then the tapestry was washed in a tub equipped with a special screen liner so the tapestry could be safely supported when hoisted out flat on the screen through soaking and rinsing steps.

Next, areas where the tapestry threads had deteriorated were restored. New warp (lengthwise) threads were put in, and fishing weights further held the threads in place to provide just the right tension for the repair work. Among repairs was the reweaving of the shadows, because the brown and black threads had deteriorated the most.

Total work time: 3,450 hours

A frame forms part of a painting's image. That is why decisions about frames are made by a committee of curators, conservators, and members of the museum's design staff. The committee examines all the frames in the museum and consider: Are they historically correct? Suited to the work? In good condition?

Original frames, still holding the paintings for which they were made, are treasured, and conservators try to preserve them as well as they can. "We're capable of making a 16th-century frame look shiny and new, but we wouldn't want to. The dirt is evidence of use and time, and that's part of its history," a conservator says. "We clean away some dirt and bring out the old gold, and we replace the missing pieces, but if the frame ends up looking old—that's how it should be."

Sometimes the framers can fit authentic old frames to paintings, and they have a storage room of them to choose from. The museum also buys frames to suit individual paintings. When necessary, the framers make frames, using old tools, materials, and techniques.

Charts of frame styles as well as samples of finishes, such as wood stains and gold leaf, are kept in the frame shop. Here, one frame conservator works at an easel to restore an old gold frame that had been patched up with bronze paint. This paint has turned brown, green, and splotchy. To remove the discolorations, the conservator uses cotton swabs dipped in solvents. A sure hand is needed to keep from ruining the gold underneath.

A conservator prepares to apply gold leaf. The tools needed, lower left, are: a suede gilder's pad, gilder's knife, gold leaf beneath sable-haired gilder's tip, and a burnisher, with rounded agate end, to smooth the gold.

In the same studio, another framer begins the long process of applying gold leaf to a new pine frame. He built the frame in the shop according to centuries-old methods.

The new frame is carved and sanded. Then its surface is prepared for the application of gold leaf: ten layers of gesso (a mixture of rabbit skin glue and powdered chalk) are applied and sanded to a smooth surface; then bole (glue mixed with fine clay) is laid on to adhere the gold to the frame. The conservator selects a bole—of red, blue, or yellow—to give the gold leaf that will be laid on top of it a warm, deep, or pale gold tone.

With a brush the framer wets the part of the frame he will work on with a solution of water and alcohol. He is ready for the gold leaf. There is a technique for lifting the gold, which comes in small books of sheets separated by powdered tissue papers, to the frame. Bare hands cannot do it. "If you pick up the gold, it clings to your fingers," says the framer. "So you use a gilder's brush, called a tip, made of fine sable or squirrel fur. "Just before picking up the gold, you touch the brush quickly to your forehead and across your hair to get a bit of oil and static electricity on it. When the brush touches the gold, the gold jumps to it, and you can lay it on the frame."

One sheet after another is overlapped on the frame. After 24 hours of drying, the frame can be polished with a burnishing tool, which has a tip of highly polished agate. Burnishing the flat gold makes it shine, though framers often like to leave part of the gold matte for contrast.

A framer's tour of favorites:

Stones or bits of mirror are embedded in some frames, and figures or symbols can be found carved in others. Lovebirds adorn the folk art portrait of Eliza Wells.

Sassetta's *Enthroned Madonna and Child* (c. 1435) has an "engaged frame," which is something like a marriage. The painting and the frame, both made of wood, were gessoed together to look like one piece, and then gilding was applied overall.

James McNeill Whistler painted a fish-scale design onto the carved wood frame for *The White Girl*. At the upper right he added a butterfly, his signature.

An unusual plaque telling the story of John Singleton Copley's *Watson and the Shark* (1778) is attached to the frame. It explains how Young Watson, swimming, was attacked three times by a shark and lost his leg; the beast was harpooned and killed; and Watson went on to become Lord Mayor of London—his life a lesson in overcoming adversity.

French frames, such as the one for Jean-Honoré Fragonard's *A Young Girl Reading* (c. 1776), became increasingly ornamented throughout the reigns of kings Louis XIII, XIV, and XV. Shells, vines, leaves, and flower patterns are carved throughout this frame, and light penetrates the open filigree sections.

Twentieth-century paintings may have no frames at all. Frank Stella's *La scienza della fiacca* (The Science of Laziness), a wall relief named after an Italian folktale, uses its own aluminum and fiberglass shapes to serve as both frame and artwork.

Frank Stella, *La scienza della fiacca*

Left to right: Abram Ross Stanley, *Eliza Wells;* Sassetta, *Madonna and Child;* James McNeill Whistler, detail of frame for *The White Girl*; John Singleton Copley, *Watson and the Shark;* Jean-Honoré Fragonard, *A Young Girl Reading*

4. Movers and Shakers

Art handlers are constantly on the move—on ladders installing or dismantling an exhibition, on the floor packing up works of art, or rigging a nine-ton sculpture of a cat. The colossal crouching cat, a jaguar carved by a sculptor who had only hard stone tools to work with, was part of an exhibition of Aztec art from Mexico. The art handlers signaled the forklift operator to hoist it very, very slowly.

Trusted to move art for the museum, these people know materials well—and how to handle them safely. Many are artists themselves. They always carry a tape measure, notebook, and pencil, for mapping their moves and jotting down their actions.

The art handlers' primary tools are:

Four-wheel dollies
to carry packing cases along the basement ramps and narrow corridors, where high mirrors help prevent traffic collisions at intersections.

A-frame carts
to move paintings or sheets of glass. When art that has been uncrated is carried on a cart, the art handler makes sure it is well braced and padded. Solid rubber wheels give a cushioned ride. They pivot and do not scuff floors.

Hand-powered lifts
to raise heavy objects (up to 1,000 pounds). They are used to hold an object steady and then to position it — in a niche or on a pedestal.

Electric lifts
to raise the art handler up, in a basket, to reach ceiling-high objects such as Titian's *Saint John the Evangelist on Patmos.*

"Cadillacs"
flat carts with padded trays, for transporting plates, medals, vases, and small sculpture, which is held in place with sandbags, padding, and acid-free tissue; also small paintings with ornate frames that must ride flat.

THIS WAY UP

Case makers in the museum's carpentry shop build cases of pine and plywood for artworks that will travel, on loan, to other museums. The finished cases are rolled down the hall to the paint shop, then to the registrar's packing room, where they are lined with foam and other padding. Here, too, symbols are stenciled on the outside of the cases: the broken goblet meaning FRAGILE, the umbrella meaning KEEP DRY, and arrows for RIDE FLAT, THIS WAY UP.

These cases are designed for safe travel. The fresh paint itself says: Take care!

When the newer East Building was under construction, the museum invited artists to create works especially for the space. Installing those works provided a challenge for the art handlers.

Henry Moore's *Knife Edge Mirror Two Piece,* a 15-ton bronze, consists of two huge parts. To install them, the art handlers prepared cement "footprints" with spikes to hold the sculpture in place. The foundry that cast the sculpture traced the bottom of the work and marked where the spikes should go. The art handlers practiced the installation with lightweight models, because the sculpture would require precise placement. Finally, a hydraulic crane lowered the sculpture into place inch by inch. It took four days.

Knife Edge Mirror Two Piece **traveled from England to Washington, D.C., by ship and flat-bed truck. The foundry where the sculpture was cast in bronze traced the bottom of each of its two parts so that two cement "footprints" could be made for it to stand on. The huge sculpture was installed by crane outside the museum.**

As a centerpiece for the new building, Alexander Calder created an enormous mobile. After the 83-year-old artist had made a wood model, he asked his assistant Paul Matisse (grandson of painter Henri Matisse) to build the full-size work of art. Matisse suggested using light-weight aluminum, the honey-combed kind found in the wings of airplanes. Calder agreed: "Go ahead and build it."

The mobile arrived at the museum in 13 flat crates. "Paul sat down with us and explained how the mobile locked together," recalls an art handler. "We assembled it piece by piece, raising the mobile a bit at a time with counterweights keeping the piece balanced while Paul made final adjustments."

"When we have to take it down every couple of years for cleaning or to make room for an exhibition," the handler says, "we use the original 19-page set of instructions for assembling and raising the mobile." This guidebook even lists the tools and materials needed: a walkie-talkie, to communicate with the winch crew on the roof; drills; Allen and crescent wrenches; extension cords and ropes; ladders, planks, dollies, and grease; counterweights, ranging from two-pound bags to 95-pound steel plates; three-sided carts; and blankets, to protect the mobile from scratches.

DUSTERS' RULES

Follow the rule that surfaces are more fragile than they look:

Alexander Calder's bent metal *Crinkly Worm* is painted with flat, easily scratched paint. Feather-dust it extra lightly.

The paint on Wayne Thiebaud's *Cakes* is thick, with a rich surface like icing. With a narrow brush, follow the artist's strokes.

George Segal's *The Dancers,* bronze figures with a rough white finish, collect dust and cobwebs fast. Take off your shoes and crawl across the platform to flick diapers over the heads and shoulders, where spiders like to spin.

Even in their glass cases, the wax figures by Edgar Degas attract dust. Clean them gently, with a sable brush.

Deliciously painted, Wayne Thiebaud's *Cakes* invites you to name the flavors of the thick, creamy frostings.

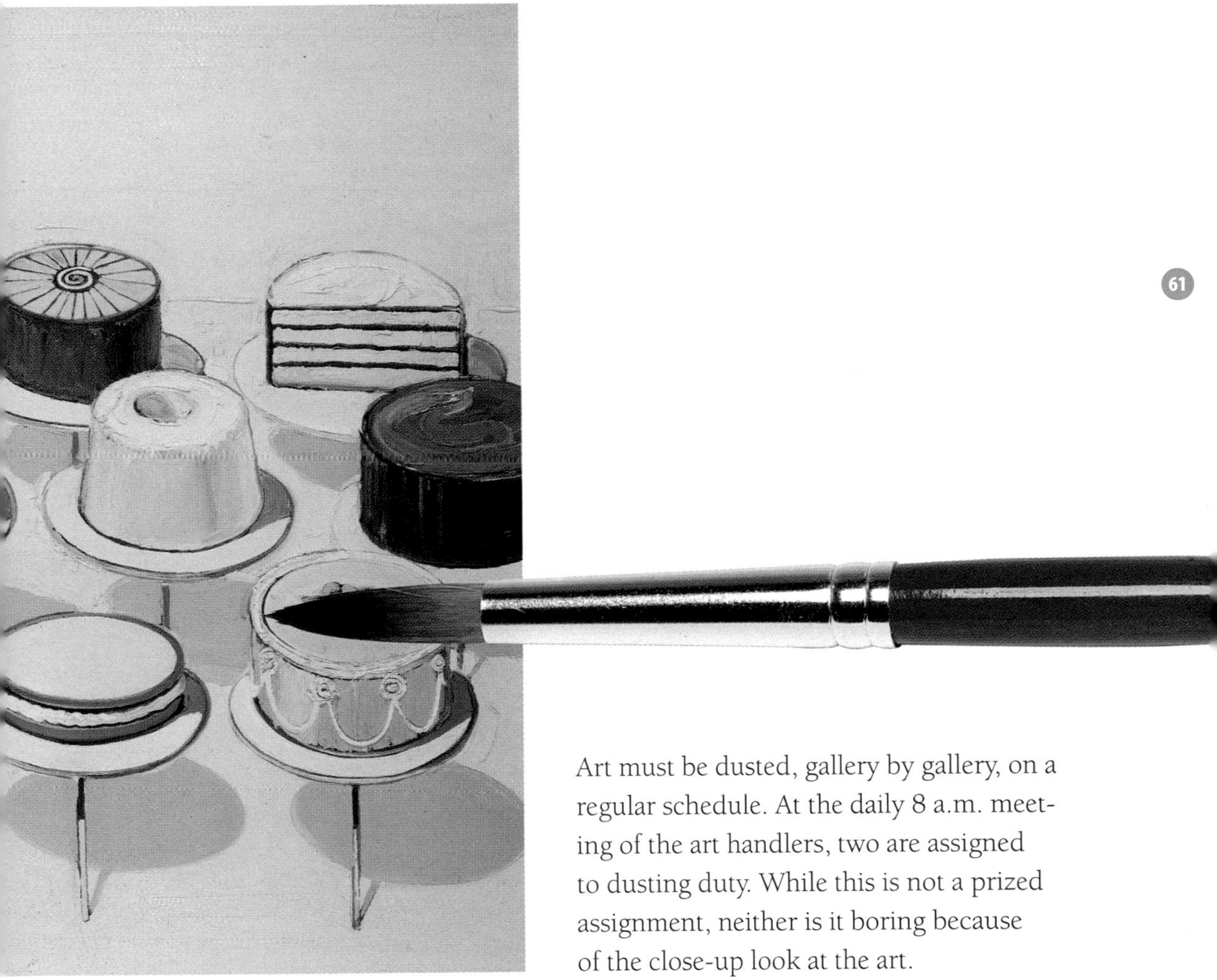

Art must be dusted, gallery by gallery, on a regular schedule. At the daily 8 a.m. meeting of the art handlers, two are assigned to dusting duty. While this is not a prized assignment, neither is it boring because of the close-up look at the art.

Starting with the painting nearest a gallery door, the pair of art handlers work their way around a room, one dusting the frames, the other dusting the surfaces of the paintings. One dusts the pedestals; the other, the sculpture. Clean, soft brushes, feather dusters, and a half-dozen cloth diapers are their tools. Pencil and notebook are always in the duster's pocket, for noting down an artwork's identification number when a scratch, mark, or other changes in condition may have appeared.

5. Art in Words

The library of this museum holds 200,000 volumes on art and art history. Books, magazines, monographs (studies of individual artists), auction catalogues, treatises on technique and art theory, and rare books focusing on Western art from the Middle Ages to the present, are stored on eight floors, five above ground and three below. With its reference room of dictionaries, encyclopedias, auction indexes, directories, and online computer access to hundreds of databases, the library is an international center for research.

When Leonardo da Vinci's portrait of *Ginevra de' Benci* was restored, the conservator in charge had 3,000 books on Leonardo right at hand, nearly everything ever written about the artist. Of special use was Leonardo's own treatise on painting, *Trattato della Pittura*. It was the artist's first published writing, issued in Italian in 1651, and the library offered 53 editions, in different languages and variously illustrated. As a writer Leonardo moved briskly from one artistic topic to another.

On the subject of light and shadow, Leonardo reminded the conservator that "The air between the eye and the object seen will change the color of that object into its own." And, famously: "The color of the shadow will never be simple."

The Italian Renaissance (1400s and 1500s) is a strength of the library, as is the period of the French impressionists (mid- to late 1800s). According to the chief librarian, catalogues from impressionist exhibitions are among the rare documents now in the library. The booklets almost had to be picked up at the time of the show. "They were just paper leaflets," he says. "Printed with the names of artists and the titles of their works, they are important for research on Renoir, Monet, Degas, and the rest of the avant-garde artists of the time."

Other library resources include diaries and scrapbooks, photographs of artists' studios, and books of pictures put together by art collectors showing where paintings now in the museum were originally hung in their homes.

Here in the library, at any given moment, readers pursue their topics. How porcelain was first made, how varnish was applied to Dutch paintings. A gold-leafer from the frame studio peruses a favorite manual written in the 1500s—*The Craftsman's Handbook* by Cennino Cennini. He likes the advice on stones to be used for burnishing gold leaf to a shine: iron ore, also sapphires, emeralds, topazes, rubies, and garnets. According to the text, a dog, lion, wolf, or cat tooth would do, too.

Documentation, advice, theory, and arguments: the library is filled with voices within its quiet, ordered shelves.

A gloved librarian opens a rare edition of Leonardo da Vinci's treatise on painting, this one in French, dated 1651. Cotton gloves protect the pages from smudges and the acidity of hands. The museum library also holds a collection of books made by artists. At left, a wooden fold-out book, handmade by Kathleen Amt, *The Mermaid.*

Peter Paul Rubens' *Daniel in the Lion's Den* and a photograph of Rubens' drawing of lions, below, from the museum's photographic archives

More than seven million photographs of works of art from all over the world are contained in the library's photo archives. The photo archivist says: "A researcher will come to us to find a history of lions in art. We'll pull out the photos to show her a carved stone lion from a Romanesque cathedral in France and other early lions from Venice or Rome.

"The earliest ones looked strange. Then they became more realistic. Ten lions are in the museum's painting of *Daniel in the Lion's Den*, by Peter Paul Rubens. We can show how Rubens used a model from classical sculpture and had studied lions in zoos before he painted the lions on his canvas."

In the historical archives, pieces of the museum's past repose in filed-away letters, clippings, drawings, diagrams, and tapes recording memories of past employees.

The archives hold the letters and memoirs of the museum's first director, David Finley, telling how Andrew Mellon had found art galleries in Europe exhausting and hoped this would not be true of Washington's National Gallery. Mellon, the founder of the museum, wanted the building to be grand but also wanted the galleries to be inviting and well lit. The floors in exhibition rooms were not to be too hard, Mellon thought. They should be of wood with a little spring, for easy walking.

When the museum first opened over 50 years ago, it seemed vast, and many rooms were nearly empty. The joke was that guards were stationed to show the way to the next painting. Some of the empty space was used as a guards' gymnasium, for basketball games.

At the start of World War II, paintings were removed from the museum and trucked over icy mountain roads to storage in North Carolina—in case bombs should fall on the city. During the war the museum put on Sunday suppers and concerts for the many service people in the city and set aside a special room where soldiers, sailors, and officers could rest and write postcards. One advised, "Not bad but needs a Coke machine."

A suitcase that belonged to the first director of the museum, with the scuffs, scratches, and stickers from his many trips abroad to study art. Also in the museum's archives, a photograph,above, of National Gallery art arriving at Biltmore House, in North Carolina, for safekeeping during World War II.

By the 1970s, the National Gallery had acquired so much art that it needed more space for its collections. Paul Mellon and Ailsa Mellon Bruce (the founder's son and daughter), made another family gift—for a new building. The archives has the story of the new East Building on tape, starting with architect I. M. Pei telling how he solved the problem of designing a museum for an odd, trapezoidal parcel of land by dividing the trapezoid diagonally to make two triangles.

Also on tape, the construction manager for the East Building recounts the challenges of the architect's design and the building's many odd angles: "Building in triangles caused chaos with the carpenters, because they're used to working with tools that are made for rectangles." Every triangle posed a challenge: setting the marble triangles into the floor; pouring concrete into wooden frames to form the coffered ceiling pieces; welding steel frames for the triangular skylight structure. Workmen on the job did not mind hearing themselves described as "artists."

STAMPED

Many of the museum's treasur objects appear on over 300 stamps of the United States ar of countries around the world, including Fiji, Yemen, Paragua and Rwanda. Among the posta stamps saved in the archives is a red, three-cent, 1955 stam honoring the National Gallery founder, Andrew Mellon, who is pictured in a tweed jacket a with his trademark mustache.

UNITED STATES POSTAGE
ANDREW W. MELLON
3¢
REPUBLIQUE DU BURUNDI
1.50 F
GUYANA South America
EASTER 1969
25c
Mary Cassatt American Artist
5c
U.S. POSTAGE
CORREO DEL PARAGUAY
G. ROMNEY
DE LA RUE DE COLOMBIA
U.S. 5c Christmas
MEMLING · NATIONAL GALLERY OF ART
28B. AIR MAIL THE MUTAWAKELITE KINGDOM OF
Christmas
Giorgione, ca. 1478-1510
National Gallery of Art
8c U.S.
10
FÜRSTENTUM LIECHTENSTEIN
5c U. S. POST
CHRISTMAS
3 Rls
RENOIR (1841-1919). Girl with Watering Can
AIR MAIL FUJEIRA
CHRISTMAS 6c
BELGIE
2F
Belgie Belgique
1c U.S. POSTAGE

6. The Protectors

Among the people who make the museum hum are the engineers who keep it warm (or cool), and humid (but not too humid); the maintenance crews who keep it clean; and the security force.

The museum sits atop a tidewater swamp. To erect the main building, workers had to drive 6,800 steel-and-concrete piers into the thick muck. These piers—think of nearly 7,000 straws in a thick milk shake—hold the building in place. Some movement of the building still occurs, to be sure, which is why the West Building consists of three separate structures: the Rotunda, with its great dome and the Mercury fountain, and beyond tiny seams that are easily seen, the two long sculpture halls, which stand to the east and west.

Over 350 miles of color-coded pipes run beneath the museum buildings.

The East Building is also afloat, on a great thick concrete platform that acts like a ship's hull and is anchored with steel cables to solid rock far below.

"Washington, D.C., is not only swampy, but also notoriously muggy," remarks the chief engineer. "It's damp most of the time, and the temperature swings from hot to cold. For art, too much humidity can be damaging. Paintings can get fungus, mold, and mildew. They need a stable environment, which is what we provide."

The museum's air systems are one part of a vast underground operating complex. In the main engine room beneath the West Building, huge piping is color coded: blue for water from the Tidal Basin, green for city water that is chilled and circulated through the buildings, and orange for the steam pipes that heat the buildings.

A hideaway office, walled off from the noise, serves as command post for the engineer overseeing the waterworks. Here, dials and blinking red and green lights trace the flow of water throughout the museum to its farthest point, four city blocks away and ten stories up, in the East Building.

FREE SHOE SHINE

The stairs in the museum's modern East Building have an unusual feature: they are designed to vacuum-clean the shoes of visitors. As fresh air enters the central court from vents in the ceiling, it is also drawn out through slots along the risers of the stairs, cleaning the shoes of visitors as they walk.

In the course of their daily rounds, engineers travel long distances underground, up and down metal stairs and through corridors like ships' passageways. They walk through low tunnels, where rows of pipes carry steam, telephone lines, drinking water, and electricity throughout the museum.

Duty calls the engineers to high places as well. Electrical problems take them to the top of the Rotunda dome by way of a ladder built into the wall; oiling the ball bearings of the Alexander Calder mobile takes them to the peak of the East Building's glass ceiling, where they hang from safety harnesses.

The National Gallery of Art's two buildings, above: the contemporary East Building, seen near the dome of the United States Capitol, and the neoclassical West Building. Left: Many of the galleries have glass ceilings, much like the skylights in an artist's studio. To clean them, workers are attached at the belt to safety wires strung high over the roof space.

The maintenance staff keeps the 1,200,000 square feet of the museum gleaming. They polish and buff, so that time and the traffic of millions of visitors will not dull the setting. They also do carpentry, painting, stone work, roof work, and glazing—to replace skylight window panes smashed by seagulls dropping stones.

Carpentry often means re-creating historical settings for art. Here, a carpenter works on the ceiling of a classical rotunda. Detail is important everywhere in the museum. At left, one of the many brass fixtures kept shining by the housekeeping staff. Right: Covering skylights to protect light-sensitive art

Carpenters put up walls and hang doors. With baffles and new walls they reshape rooms for exhibitions. In the East Building, with its odd angles, they must make angled furniture such as desks, work stations, and shelves for the staff.

Masons replace cracked cobblestones on the plaza between the buildings and repair sidewalks and marble walls. They know how to remove the East Building's glass front wall when a work of art as large as a Miró tapestry will not fit through the door.

Housekeepers operate a fleet of 30 vacuum cleaners, including one that freezes chewing gum on carpets and then rubs it out with pumice stone.

"We wax and buff," says the head housekeeper. "But we don't put down a sealer over the wax because who would want a high shine throwing reflections onto the art? We never touch the art or even the pedestals or frames. That's for conservators or art handlers. But being this close to the art is definitely something special."

A jeweler's safe with swinging doors, hooks, numbers, and secret drawers holds the 800 keys that are given out to the guards and collected again daily. The keys unlock storage rooms, offices, file cabinets, desks, cash registers, and vehicles — and 1,250 doors. The keys are cut with special machinery so they cannot be copied, and many of the locks require a combination of keys to open them.

More than 300 people are the museum's security force—among them guards, locksmiths, electronics experts, and technicians.

In a console room underground, the security staff monitors the safety of the art (Are paintings and sculpture where they are supposed to be?), the visitors (Are they entering "staff only" areas?), and the perimeters of the buildings.

Protecting the art is not easy. "We keep our valuables—works of art—out in the open," says a security staff member. "People are supposed to be drawn to the objects but not see our cameras. We hide our security devices in the ceilings and walls, behind paintings, inside doors and light fixtures. We have to provide 100 percent security but keep it inconspicuous.

"Motion detectors tell us when people are in the wrong place. With our system, we can follow a person's movements from one end of the West Building to the other. We also have cameras that work in complete darkness. They'll show us a room as if it were noon."

Enjoying his secrets, the technician says, "Even if you can't see our work, assume we are there."

The guards in their blue and gray uniforms know all about locks and alarms, but they are also trained to preserve the safety of the art and the people in the buildings.

"Though we must enforce the Gallery's rules, we learn to do it in a low-key way," a guard says.

"Long hours of guard duty can be hard on knees and feet. Our posts get shifted around, so we're not in the same space each day. Assignments are given out in the morning at a 9:15 roll call. We can be in the East Building on Monday and the west end of the West Building on Tuesday, but the routine is always the same. At the start of duty, count everything in your rooms; at the end, count it again.

"The most desirable post is the French impressionist rooms," the guard adds. "It's lively—a lot of people come through, and they're smiling, talking, relaxed. At first we didn't like working in the East Building, because we didn't know 20th-century art. We'd see a raw canvas and swats of paint. That's how it looked to us. It didn't help when a visitor would tell us: 'My kid can do better than that!'

"Then the 20th-century curators came in at morning roll call and helped us understand the art. They explained that it was just the same in the 1800s when the public first saw French impressionist paintings. People made fun of the everyday subjects—the laundress and café scenes—and they were offended by the artists' loose brushwork, which they thought looked like spots and streaks. The curators absolutely turned us around."

This officer likes the busiest days best. Most do, she says. She likes responding to visitors' questions: Where's the Metro station? The café? Vermeer? "Those days rush by."

A guard stands before a painting by Robert Motherwell and a floor sculpture made of slate by Richard Long. In the 20th-century galleries, she is asked many questions about the art itself. At left, the nerve center of security operations, where television monitors help track art and visitors

7. Paradise Gardening

In Rembrandt Peale's portrait of his teenage brother, the geranium—the first plant of its kind in America—is painted as lovingly as the young man. People stand before this painting, fascinated. It speaks to them. It speaks to the museum horticulture staff, too, but in a different way. The head of the horticulture staff says: "We wish Rubens Peale would water his geranium!"

Early in the morning, the gardeners mist, feed, trim, spray, and water the plants throughout the museum. The museum's low light is hard on plants, and the four large ficus trees in the East Building must be continually turned toward the window light. Heaving together, the gardeners give each tree a quarter of a turn clockwise every two months.

Top: Installing large ficus trees in the East Building requires precision and the assistance of a crane. Displays of plants and flowers, below, change seasonally.

Nine greenhouses hidden from public view welcome the plants home after duty in the museum. One greenhouse is reserved for azaleas—more than 100 varieties, many with pedigrees. The greenhouses are also stocked with hardy plants that do well in low light and low humidity—herbs, ivies, begonias, and fishtail palm trees. Some of the tall palms in the garden courts have longer employment records than the gardeners.

Among the 15,000 plants in the museum: a group of Greek myrtle (*Myrtus communis*) topiaries in one of the greenhouses; the famous azalea collection, viewed from high in the dome; and a Japanese teahouse and garden created for an exhibition of Japanese culture

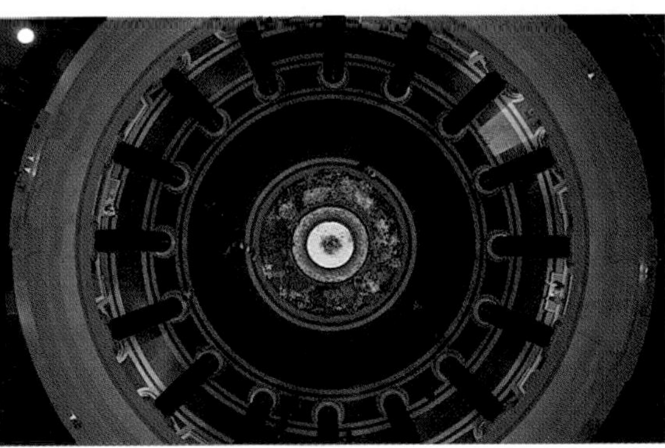

Great care is taken with the greenhouses because the plants serve many purposes. Their colors and textures create mood, and plants grouped together form screens behind sculpture or help direct visitors. Plants also hide construction in progress.

For special exhibitions the horticulturists plan ahead to obtain plants that reflect the style or period of the works of art. For an exhibition of paintings made by Matisse in Morocco, the gardeners assembled masses of yellow and pink lantanas, oleanders, hibiscus, jasmine, and palms. "No plant should stand out or call attention to itself," a gardener says. "You just want to create the atmosphere. You want everything together to say tropical paradise."

One of the gardeners' triumphs was creating an authentic Japanese garden for an exhibition on the arts of feudal Japan. All around a thatched-roof teahouse, they built a four-foot-wide platform, laid a stone walkway on it, and edged it with Japanese grass, hollies, pines, and bamboo.

For an exhibition of ancient Greek sculpture, the gardeners chose fragrant herbs—rosemary and lavender, which abound in Greece—and acanthus, with its huge shining leaves. Acanthus leaves, carved in stone, appeared in the show's sculpture at the tops of columns and in border designs.

Gerard David, ***The Rest on the Flight into Egypt***

wild strawberry

fern

violet

THE NAME OF THE FLOWER

Horticulture plays a role in understanding the meaning (iconography) of a work of art. In Gerard David's *The Rest on the Flight into Egypt,* the plant life eyed by the donkey is nondescript, but the plants at the feet of the Madonna and Child are specific: wild straw-berry, a fern, and a violet. The three-leaved strawberry was a Christian symbol for the trinity of Father, Son, and Holy Ghost. The fern was regarded as protection against evil, and the violet signified the humility of the Virgin Mary and her child.

8. The Need to Know

*Refined…Barbaric…Perfectly truthful…A skinny rat….*A lecturer, intent over a book in the library, jots down comments that were made a century ago about a sculpture by Edgar Degas, *Little Dancer Fourteen Years Old* (1878/1881). She is reading about the French impressionist artist for a tour she will lead with fifth-graders the next day. She has given this lecture many times but wants to verify some facts.

The girl who posed for the artist, Marie van Goethem, attended children's ballet classes at the Paris Opéra. Now she stands fixed in fourth position, hands clasped behind her back, eyes half closed, chin thrust forward, a braid trailing down her back. Degas originally modeled her in flesh-tinted wax to which he affixed a wig, silk hair ribbon, bodice, gauze tutu, and actual ballet slippers. When the *Little Dancer*—so coltish and alive—was exhibited in Paris in 1881, it caused a commotion among art critics and viewers.

The lecturer asks the fifth-graders the next day to look closely at the plaster version of the sculpture as she recounts the critics' remarks, and to form their own opinions. The students have lots of ideas.

"Bony, almost puny," says one.

"No, she's tough. Look at her muscles," says another student, a dancer herself. "I bet she worked hard on her dance."

A third student steps back and crosses her arms. "She's thinking not to mess up."

By the time the students finish discussing the dancer, they have debated the implications of one critic's backhanded remark: "In this nasty little figure...there is...something which comes of an observant and loyal artist...the perfect truthfulness of gesture...."

Degas probably had the small bodice and ballet slippers made to order for the original *Little Dancer,* which was of wax.

That is the job of the education staff and volunteers: to engage people in considering and understanding art. Museum educators are aware that they must be sensitive to what different visitors want to know and how they learn. Curators develop scholarship about art, but it is the educators' responsibility to share it with visitors. While some people are new to looking at art, others may have a lifetime of experience and want to see and learn much more.

More than 4 million people a year visit the museum. In addition to tours and lectures, given in six languages, activities are planned for children.

Young visitors consider Claes Oldenburg's *Typewriter Eraser*, above. On a snowy morning, visitors, at right, line up to see a special exhibit of paintings by 17th-century Dutch artist Johannes Vermeer; and two visitors study works of art through an interactive computer program.

Volunteers and staff at art information desks answer questions. For a general visit, they might recommend a selection of ten paintings and tell visitors about the tours and lectures.

The education department develops guides to the meaning, style, and context of works of art. In addition, an interactive computer program, the Micro Gallery, lets visitors design personal tours and includes pathways for learning about the history, conservation and varied interpretations of artworks in the museum.

The name means what it says: the National Gallery of Art belongs to the American people, and programs about art are lent free to those who cannot come to the museum.

A painter copies Rembrandt's *The Mill* in one of the Dutch galleries, top; and a museum volunteer, or docent, leads a tour.

A ceremonial Arapaho dress, above, decorated with symbols of nature and the cosmos. Below, an Indian shirt made of buckskin and the quills or hair of a porcupine, horses, and humans. Printed pairs of hands show that the owner was a brave warrior who engaged in hand-to-hand combat with enemies. The Iroquois moccasins, at far right, were made in the early 19th century.

The education department also interprets exhibitions. For *Art of the American Indian Frontier: The Collecting of Chandler and Pohrt,* the staff developed programs and information that connected visitors with the art and the meanings of American Indian objects.

In the 1920s, two young men, who lived near American Indian reservations in the Midwest, became friends with members of several tribes. They received gifts and also purchased objects from the Indians. Intrigued by the beauty and meaning of the Indian buckskin shoulder bags, wooden pipe bowls, feather bonnets, and rawhide shields, Milford Chandler and Richard Pohrt became collectors of American Indian art. Seventy years later, their collection spent two months on view in the museum.

To plan programs the staff met with the show's curator. "Americans' concept of the frontier often leaves out the Indians' perspective," the curator explained. "Many of the objects selected show how the Indians' rich culture was tied to their environment and also reflected their response to the harsh circumstances of losing their land."

Keeping in mind these points of view and the cultural meanings of the objects, the education staff began work. A symposium, a lecture series, films by and about American Indians, teaching packets, and storytelling sessions were organized.

At the symposium someone asked: What happens to the spiritual meaning of an Indian object when it is removed from its tribal setting and placed in a museum? Example: a vibrant Arapaho dress on display in the exhibition. It was worn in a ceremony called the Ghost Dance, which Indians on a Sioux reservation hoped could restore the world they once knew. Chief Sitting Bull was killed, in part, for his support of the dance, which the government viewed as a threat of insurrection; shortly thereafter, in 1890, an entire band of Ghost Dancers were killed at Wounded Knee, South Dakota. The dress was made for a dancer who moved in a circle with others to summon the forces of abundance and hope. Motionless behind glass, the dress appeared far different than it had during a firelit ceremony.

The group discussed the details of the dress, which represent the sky and the spirit world with a cedar tree at the hem, the sun and moon at the shoulders, and crows flying skyward with messages. They agreed that though muted, the famous dress seems to carry a message about faith and hope across the generations.

Six p.m.

At a work table five floors up in the museum, plans are being laid out—pictures, outlines, ideas—for a book about the museum. This book will invite readers behind the scenes into the museum's private spaces, the workshops, offices, and labs where visitors rarely enter. It will begin with a guard patrolling in the early morning dark, a lamper, some art handlers, a curator arranging pictures in a gallery, and the first splashes of a fountain coming to life.

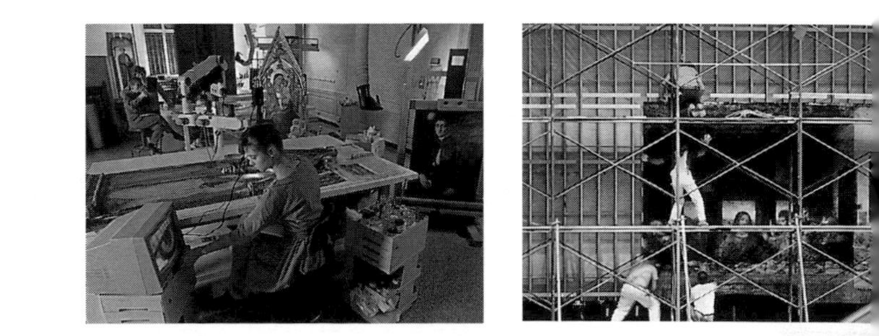

Picture Credits

All works of art are in the collections of the National Gallery of Art, Washington, except as noted.

FRONT COVER
Aztec
Colossal jaguar cuauhxicalli
Andesite
Museo Nacional de Antropología, Mexico City

BACK COVER
Andrea del Verrocchio
Putto Poised on a Globe
probably 1480
Unbaked clay
Andrew W. Mellon Collection

PAGE 10
Jean Dubuffet
Site à l'homme assis, 1969–1984
Polyester resin
Gift of Robert M. and Anne T. Bass and Arnold and Mildred Glimcher, in Honor of the 50th Anniversary of the National Gallery of Art

PAGE 15
(TOP)
Jean-Baptiste Oudry
The Marquis de Beringhen, 1722
Oil on canvas
Eugene L. and Marie-Louise Garbáty Fund, Patrons' Permanent Fund and Chester Dale Fund

(BOTTOM)
Jean-Baptiste Oudry
Misse and Luttine, 1729
Oil on canvas
Gift of Mr. and Mrs. Eugene Victor Thaw, in Honor of the 50th Anniversary of the National Gallery of Art

PAGE 16
Hieronymus Bosch
Death and the Miser, c.1485/1490
Oil on panel
Samuel H. Kress Collection

PAGE 21
Paul Gauguin
Pair of Wooden Shoes, 1889
Wood, polychromed, and leather
Chester Dale Collection

PAGE 23
Albert Bierstadt
Lake Lucerne, 1858
Oil on canvas
Gift of Richard M. Scaife and Margaret R. Battle, in Honor of the 50th Anniversary of the National Gallery of Art

PAGE 29
Edward Savage
The Washington Family, 1789–1796
Oil on canvas
Andrew W. Mellon Collection

PAGE 30
Mark Leithauser, plan for fireplace installation, *The Treasure Houses of Britain: 500 Years of Private Patronage and Art Collecting* (National Gallery of Art, 3 November 1985–13 April 1986)

PAGES 32–33
Aztec
Colossal jaguar cuauhxicalli
Andesite
Museo Nacional de Antropología, Mexico City

PAGE 34
(LEFT TO RIGHT)
Chalice of the Abbot Suger of Saint-Denis, 2nd/1st century B.C. (cup); 1137–1140 (mounting)
Sardonyx cup with gilded silver mounting, and filigrees set with stones, pearls, glass insets, and white glass pearls
Widener Collection

Jasper Johns
Field Painting, 1963/1964
Oil with objects on canvas
Collection of the Artist

Andrea del Verrocchio
Lorenzo de' Medici, c. 1478
Terracotta, painted
Samuel H. Kress Collection

PAGE 35
Andrea del Verrocchio
Putto Poised on a Globe
probably 1480
Unbaked clay
Andrew W. Mellon Collection

Henri Matisse
La Négresse, 1952
Collage on canvas
Ailsa Mellon Bruce Fund

PAGE 38
Leonardo da Vinci
Ginevra de' Benci, c. 1474
Oil on panel
Ailsa Mellon Bruce Fund

PAGE 45
Boas Ulrich
Coffer, c. 1595/1600
Ebony and ebony veneer over spruce and walnut, with silver and gilded silver mounts
Samuel H. Kress Collection

PAGE 47
Edgar Degas
Seated Woman Wiping Her Left Hip, probably 1901/1911
Brown wax
Collection of Mr. and Mrs. Paul Mellon

PAGE 49
Netherlandish, 16th Century
The Triumph of Christ ("Mazarin" Tapestry), c. 1495–1500
Tapestry: undyed wool warp; dyed wool and silk, and silver-gilt and silver-wrapped silk weft
Widener Collection

PAGE 52
(LEFT TO RIGHT)
Abram Ross Stanley
Eliza Wells, 1840
Oil on canvas
Gift of Edgar William and Bernice Chrysler Garbisch

Sassetta
Madonna and Child, c. 1435
Tempera on panel
Samuel H. Kress Collection

James McNeill Whistler
Detail, frame, *The White Girl (Symphony in White, No. 1)*, 1862
Harris Whittemore Collection

PAGE 53
(TOP)
Frank Stella
La scienza della fiacca (The Science of Laziness), 1984
Oil, urethane enamel, fluorescent alkyd, acrylic, and printing ink on canvas, etched magnesium, aluminum, and fiberglass
Robert and Jane Meyerhoff Collection

(BOTTOM, LEFT TO RIGHT)
John Singleton Copley
Watson and the Shark, 1778
Oil on canvas
Ferdinand Lammot Belin Fund

Jean-Honoré Fragonard
A Young Girl Reading, c. 1776
Oil on canvas
Gift of Mrs. Mellon Bruce in Memory of Her Father, Andrew W. Mellon

PAGE 57
Henry Moore
Knife Edge Mirror Two Piece 1977/1978
Bronze
Gift of the Morris and Gwendolyn Cafritz Foundation

PAGES 60–61
Wayne Thiebaud
Cakes, 1963
Oil on canvas
Gift in Honor of the 50th Anniversary of the National Gallery of Art from the Collectors Committee, the 50th Anniversary Gift Committee, and The Circle, with Additional Support from the Abrams Family in Memory of Harry N. Abrams

PAGE 64
Kathleen Amt
The Mermaid, 1989
Wood, with colored polymer onlays

PAGE 66
(TOP)
Sir Peter Paul Rubens
Daniel in the Lions' Den
c. 1613/1615
Oil on canvas
Ailsa Mellon Bruce Fund

(BOTTOM)
Sir Peter Paul Rubens
Two Lions
Pen and ink on paper
By courtesy of the Board of Trustees of the Victoria and Albert Museum, London

PAGE 79
Rembrandt Peale
Rubens Peale with a Geranium
1801
Oil on canvas
Patrons' Permanent Fund

PAGE 82
Gerard David
The Rest on the Flight into Egypt
c. 1510
Oil on panel
Andrew W. Mellon Collection

PAGES 85,86
Edgar Degas
Little Dancer Fourteen Years Old
(Petite danseuse de quatorze ans)
1878–1881
Yellow wax, linen bodice covered with wax, muslin tutu, satin shoes covered with wax, and satin ribbon
Collection of Mr. and Mrs. Paul Mellon, Upperville, Virginia

PAGE 90
Arapaho Dress
Oklahoma, c.1890
Buckskin, feathers, pigment
Buffalo Bill Historical Center, Cody, Wyoming

Mandan Man's Shirt, c.1880
Buckskin, wool, stroud, porcupine quills, human hair, horsehair, and pigment
Richard and Marion Pohrt Collection
Photograph © Robert Hensleigh

PAGE 91
Iroquois Moccasins, New York State or Ontario, 1800–1830
Buckskin, wool fabric, porcupine quills, and glass beads
Detroit Institute of Arts, Founders Society Purchase with Funds from the Flint Ink Corporation

Photographs

Dennis Brack/Black Star: pages 6, 8 (lower left),12, 14, 20, 24, 27 (top), 28 (lower left), 36, 39, 42 (bottom), 44 (bottom), 48, 54, 55 (left), 57 (lower right), 62, 65, 70, 71, 72, 73, 74 (bottom), 75, 76, 77, 78, 80 (bottom), 81 (bottom), 87, 88 (lower right), 89, 92, 93 (left)

Kathleen Buckalew: pages 8 (upper left and lower right), 9, 11, 26, 27 (bottom), 44 (top), 55 (right), 81 (right)

James Pipkin: front cover

William Schaeffer: pages 28-29, 30-31, 32-33, 74 (top)

Robert Shelley: pages 1, 8 (upper right), 10, 42-43 (with Philip Charles), 50 (with Philip Charles), 50-51, 88 (bottom)

Kathleen Walsh-Piper: page 84

Additional photography by Dean Beasom, Richard Carafelli, Philip Charles, Lorene Emerson, and Bob Grove of the Visual Services Department, National Gallery of Art